Granny's Purses

Holly Williams

Granny's Purses

iUniverse books may be ordered through booksellers or by contacting:

iUniverse
1663 Liberty Drive
Bloomington, IN 47403
www.iuniverse.com
844-349-9409

Because of the dynamic nature of the Internet, any web addresses or links contained in this book may have changed since publication and may no longer be valid. The views expressed in this work are solely those of the author and do not necessarily reflect the views of the publisher, and the publisher hereby disclaims any responsibility for them.

Any people depicted in stock imagery provided by Getty Images are models, and such images are being used for illustrative purposes only.
Certain stock imagery © Getty Images.

ISBN: 978-1-6632-2682-2 (sc)
       978-1-6632-2683-9 (hc)
       978-1-6632-2684-6 (e)

Library of Congress Control Number: 2021914808

Print information available on the last page.

iUniverse rev. date: 07/22/2021

Granny's Purses

Dedicated to my grannies and great grannies

LW, BKWB, MFRC, MPC

In memory of:

YMBA, MIBP

To my lovely Mother and Nana to seventeen grandchildren and twelve great grandchildren.

To my wonderful family and friends for your unwavering love and support and my illustrator (Olivia) for your patience and the iUniverse team.

Purses are carried by many different people
in many different places and in many
different ways all over the world.

Purses come in different sizes, colors,
materials, shapes, styles and designs

Granny would sometimes call her purses a crossbody bag,
a pocketbook, handbag, a clutch, a grip and a tote.

A purse can be defined as a bag to carry
money and/or personal items.

Granny would carry her purse while
wearing her Sunday's best

as a crossbody bag while
walking in the park

going on a date
with grandpa

shopping for groceries

walking her dogs

playing cards with friends

being granny of the bride

waiting for the bus

going to work

night on the town

visiting granny

simply holding our hands
as we cross the street.

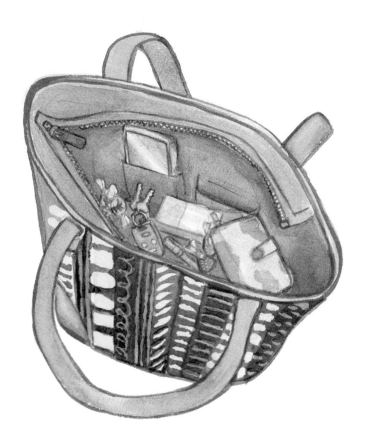

Can you name some things in granny's purse?

1. _____

2. _____

3. _____

4. _____

5. _____

Can you draw a purse?

"Dreams become reality for those who believe"

Printed in the United States
by Baker & Taylor Publisher Services